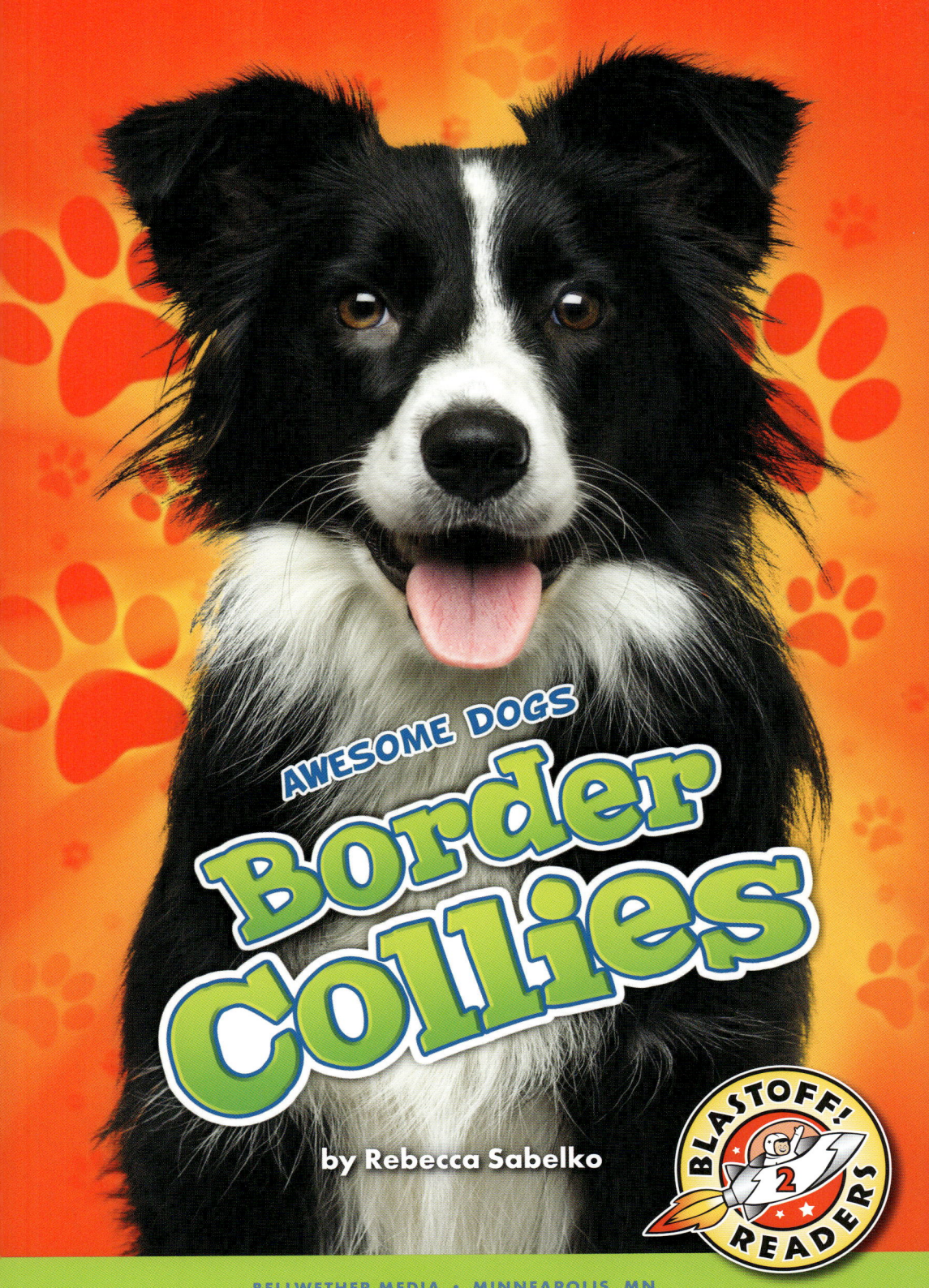

AWESOME DOGS
Border Collies

by Rebecca Sabelko

Note to Librarians, Teachers, and Parents:

Blastoff! Readers are carefully developed by literacy experts and combine standards-based content with developmentally appropriate text.

Level 1 provides the most support through repetition of high-frequency words, light text, predictable sentence patterns, and strong visual support.

Level 2 offers early readers a bit more challenge through varied simple sentences, increased text load, and less repetition of high-frequency words.

Level 3 advances early-fluent readers toward fluency through increased text and concept load, less reliance on visuals, longer sentences, and more literary language.

Level 4 builds reading stamina by providing more text per page, increased use of punctuation, greater variation in sentence patterns, and increasingly challenging vocabulary.

Level 5 encourages children to move from "learning to read" to "reading to learn" by providing even more text, varied writing styles, and less familiar topics.

Whichever book is right for your reader, Blastoff! Readers are the perfect books to build confidence and encourage a love of reading that will last a lifetime!

This edition first published in 2018 by Bellwether Media, Inc.

No part of this publication may be reproduced in whole or in part without written permission of the publisher. For information regarding permission, write to Bellwether Media, Inc., Attention: Permissions Department, 5357 Penn Avenue South, Minneapolis, MN 55419.

Library of Congress Cataloging-in-Publication Data

Names: Sabelko, Rebecca, author.
Title: Border Collies / by Rebecca Sabelko.
Other titles: Blastoff! Readers. 2, Awesome Dogs.
Description: Minneapolis, MN : Bellwether Media, Inc., [2018] | Series: Blastoff! Readers: Awesome Dogs | Audience: Ages 5-8. | Audience: K to Grade 3. | Includes bibliographical references and index.
Identifiers: LCCN 2017028762 | ISBN 9781626177406 (hardcover : alk. paper) | ISBN 9781681034553 (ebook)
Subjects: LCSH: Border collie--Juvenile literature.
Classification: LCC SF429.B64 S23 2018 | DDC 636.737/4--dc23
LC record available at https://lccn.loc.gov/2017028762

Text copyright © 2018 by Bellwether Media, Inc. BLASTOFF! READERS and associated logos are trademarks and/or registered trademarks of Bellwether Media, Inc. SCHOLASTIC, CHILDREN'S PRESS, and associated logos are trademarks and/or registered trademarks of Scholastic Inc., 557 Broadway, New York, NY 10012.

Editor: Betsy Rathburn   Designer: Tamara JM Peterson

Printed in the United States of America, North Mankato, MN.

Table of Contents

What Are Border Collies?	4
Dogs of Many Colors	8
History of Border Collies	12
Busy Buddies	18
Glossary	22
To Learn More	23
Index	24

What Are Border Collies?

Border collies are energetic dogs. They love to work and learn.

They are among the smartest dogs in the world!

Border collies are **alert**. Their ears stand straight up at the smallest sounds.

Border Collie Profile

pointy ears
oval-shaped eyes
double coat

Life Span: 10 to 17 years

Trainability:

| 1 | 2 | 3 | 4 | 5 | 6 |

Hardest to train — Easiest to train

These dogs have medium-sized bodies. They are strong and fast.

Dogs of Many Colors

Some border collies have rough **coats**. Their fur is long and **coarse**. Other border collies have short, smooth coats.

rough coats

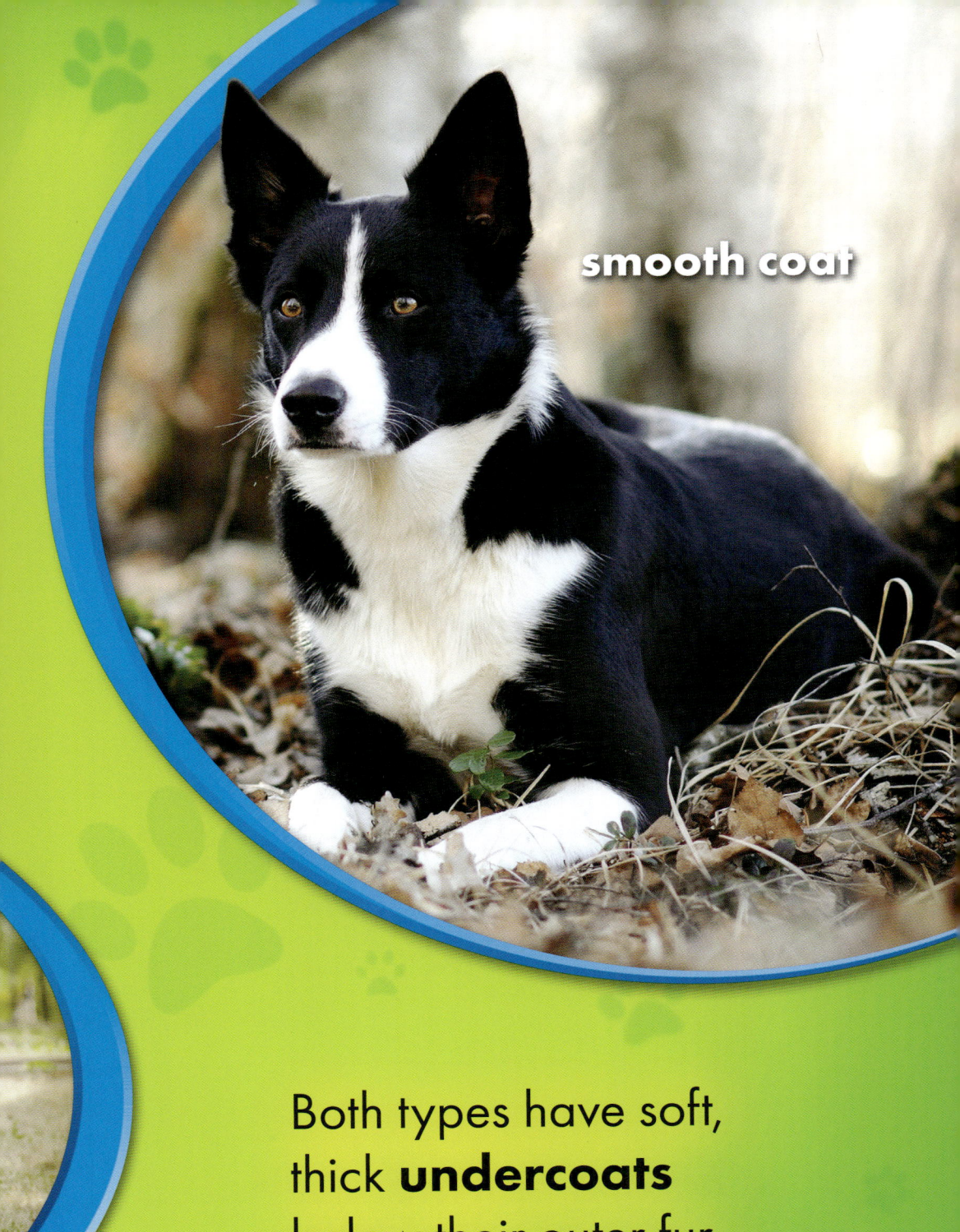

smooth coat

Both types have soft, thick **undercoats** below their outer fur.

merle

Border collies come in many colors and patterns. **Merle** and **ticked** dogs are popular.

Border Collie Coats

black and white   red and white

Other border collies may be black and white or red and white.

History of Border Collies

Border collies are sheepdogs that have helped farmers for hundreds of years.

These dogs first lived near the border between England and Scotland. This is how the **breed** got its name.

Farmers taught the dogs to follow hand **signals** and whistles to herd sheep. This impressed many people.

Later, dog shows showed off the breed's **intelligence**.

Border collies joined the **Herding Group** of the **American Kennel Club** in 1995.

They still wow crowds with their tricks!

Busy Buddies

Border collies love to stay busy.
They need a lot of space to run.

They are happiest while herding or competing in **agility** events.

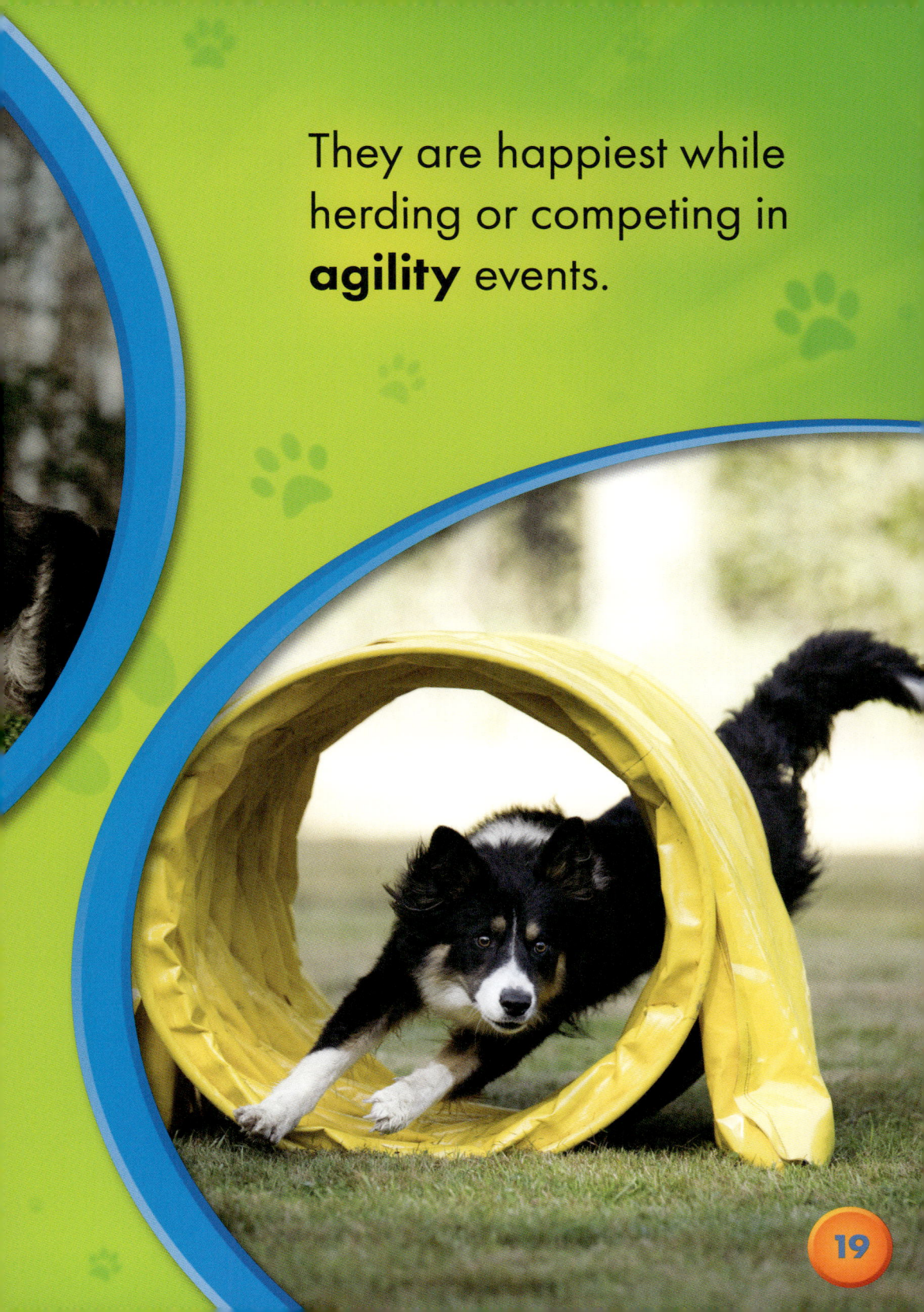

Border collies are family dogs. They like to be near people.

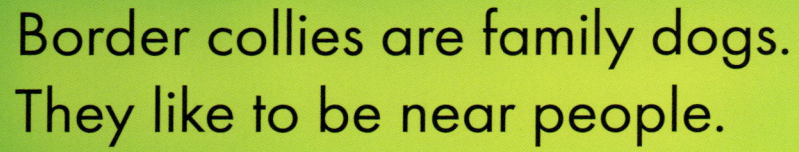

These dogs make great furry friends!

Glossary

agility—a dog sport where dogs run through a series of obstacles

alert—quick to notice or act

American Kennel Club—an organization that keeps track of dog breeds in the United States

breed—a type of dog

coarse—rough

coats—the hair or fur covering some animals

Herding Group—a group of dog breeds that like to control the movement of other animals

intelligence—the ability to learn and be trained

merle—a pattern that is one solid color with patches and spots of another color

signals—words or actions that give directions

ticked—a coat made of hairs that have two or more lines of colors

undercoats—layers of short, soft hair or fur that keep some dog breeds warm

To Learn More

AT THE LIBRARY

Gagne, Tammy. *Collies, Corgies, and Other Herding Dogs*. North Mankato, Minn.: Capstone Press, 2017.

Gray, Susan H. *Border Collies*. New York, NY.: AV2 by Weigl, 2017.

Schuh, Mari. *Collies*. Minneapolis, Minn.: Bellwether Media, 2018.

ON THE WEB

Learning more about border collies is as easy as 1, 2, 3.

1. Go to www.factsurfer.com.

2. Enter "border collies" into the search box.

3. Click the "Surf" button and you will see a list of related web sites.

With factsurfer.com, finding more information is just a click away.

Index

agility, 19
alert, 6
American Kennel Club, 16
bodies, 7
breed, 13, 15
coats, 7, 8, 9, 10, 11
colors, 10, 11
dog shows, 15
ears, 6, 7
England, 13
eyes, 7
family, 20
farmers, 12, 14
friends, 21
fur, 8, 9
hand signals, 14
herding, 14, 19
Herding Group, 16
intelligence, 5, 15
learn, 4
life span, 7
name, 13
patterns, 10

Scotland, 13
sheepdogs, 12
size, 7
trainability, 7
tricks, 17
undercoats, 9
whistles, 14
work, 4

The images in this book are reproduced through the courtesy of: Eric Isselee, front cover, pp. 4, 7, 11 (left, right); Grigorita Ko, p. 5; Lobstrosity, pp. 6-7, 14-15; Ksenia Raykova, pp. 8-9; Tierfotoagentur/ A. Geier/ Alamy, p. 9; Dora Zett, pp. 10-11; lidian Neeleman, pp. 12-13; stockcam, p. 14; Runa Kazakova, pp. 16, 18-19; vikarus, p. 17; Angelique van Heertum, p. 19; Jan Mlkvy, pp. 20-21; Heather Katz, p. 21.